Amazon Echo
The Ultimate Beginner's Guide to Amazon Echo (Alexa Skills Kit, Amazon Echo 2016, user manual, web services, Free books, Free Movie, Alexa Kit)

ANDREW BUTLER

ISBN: 1539473589

ISBN-13: 978-1539473589

CONTENTS

Introduction

The Amazon Echo is a new, revolutionary voice-activated, feature rich interface, Bluetooth speaker, streaming device and smart home controller. With powerful voice-recognition capability, cloud connectivity and wireless access to Wi-Fi–– the Amazon Echo offers users erstwhile unimagined interactivity between technology and daily life. The Amazon Echo represents a new paradigm of interactive artificial intelligence; connecting users to their homes with a variety of options from interior lighting operations to full control of TV and sound systems––all of which are commanded by voice-activation. The Amazon Echo is a single device capable of retrieving information instantly; it offers users wide access to a wealth of custom features and merges media devices into one stunning interface.

Amazon Echo is undeniable a step into the future. Originally released in November 2015, Echo has already developed in leaps and bounds. With Amazon and individual developers continuously evolving the cloud-based voice recognition software, Alexa. There is no doubt about it, there's lot to envy about Echo.

The digital assistant that is Alexa will help you organize your life in a variety of aspects. Alexa can manage your alarms, calendars and to-do lists.

There's plenty more to learn about Alexa, including how Echo can integrate with your smart home devices. In this simple guide we will teach you all about the basics and supply you with exactly what you need to say to get to grips with Alexa. Step into the world of Alexa and 'hands-free' your life in more ways than you can imagine.

Amazon has really stepped up to the plate with their new device: Amazon Echo. It looks like a speaker, but once it is experienced firsthand, it's safe to say that it is definitely more than a speaker. There really isn't a word to describe what it truly is.

Here is a brief description of what the Echo can do: play music from one of many of your favorite music apps, answer questions, give info on local businesses, provide sports scores and schedules, control lights, switches, and thermostats, listen from across the room with far-field voice recognition, and that's not all of it. The Echo is unimaginable. It's similar to a smartphone, but it is designed specifically for one's home.

If it's like a smartphone, what's the point of purchasing it? Well, the idea of the Echo can make it seem like a smartphone, but it's not a smartphone. It can do all the functions that a smartphone can do but faster, better, and to be honest, it is more capable than a smartphone. However, unlike a smartphone, the Echo can't make phone calls. At least not yet at the time of this writing, that is. Right now it is able to send emails and texts. Sounds impossible, right? But somehow Amazon has made it possible.

Amazon Echo is considered to be the next big thing because of its quick popularity since its release to the public. It's also said to be the next billion-dollar business for Amazon. Some are inquiring how a speaker can make a company become a billion-dollar business. And that's actually not a hard question to answer. Again, it's all about the details.

Chapter 1: Getting Started: The Basics

Set Up

Amazon Echo is built for a simple, sharp and seamless set up.

First things first, before you install your Echo at home, **download the Alexa App**. Free to download from appropriate app stores or from http://alexa.amazon.com for desktop users. The Alexa App will let you change a variety of settings with your Echo and is the secondary way to communicate with Alexa.

Once you've downloaded the Alexa App, install Echo into your home. Find a **suitable location** that meets the requirements - at least 8 inches (20cm) from any walls, windows or other electronic devices that could cause interference (e.g. your microwave). Once Echo is homed, plug the adapter in and then connect to the power outlet.

Echo's light ring will glow blue before turning orange at which point Alexa will greet you.

Next, **connect to Wi-Fi**. Echo can't connect to mobile hotspots or Ad-hoc (peer to peer) networks. Follow the next steps to connect your Echo with a Wi-Fi network.

1) Open the Alexa App > Open the left-hand-side navigation panel > Choose *Settings* from the options > Select your device > Choose *Set up a new device.*

2) On your Echo device press and hold the *Action* button for 5 seconds. This will change the Light Ring to orange whilst your device connects.

3) Return to the Alexa App - a list of Wi-Fi networks available for you to connect to will appear. If your

Network does not appear choose *Rescan* or *Add a Network* from the bottom of the list.

Before you start using Alexa, **choose your wake word.** Your wake word is how Alexa knows you want/need something. The default settings mean Echo will respond to Alexa but if you want to you can change this to either Echo or Amazon. To do this follow these steps:

1) Open the Alexa App > Open the left-hand-side navigation panel > Select *Settings* > Choose your device> Scroll through the options> Select *Wake Word* > From the drop down menu chose your

desired wake word > Select Save >The light ring will briefly flash orange.

The Light Ring

To visually communicate with you, Echo has a light ring situated on its top. Beaming light in a variety of colors and arrangements, Echo can visually display Alexa's status. See the table below for some of Echo's light ring codes.

Color or Light Arrangement Visible	What this means
Solid blue with spinning cyan lights	Echo is starting up
All lights off	Echo is active and ready for requests
Orange light spinning clockwise	Echo is connecting to your Wi-Fi network

Continuous oscillating violet light	An error occurred during Wi-Fi setup.
Solid red light	The microphones are off. (Press the microphone button to turn on the microphones.)
White light	You are adjusting Echo's volume level.

Power LED

Also situated at the top of Echo is the Power Led. This visually shares Echo's Wi-Fi connection status with you. A solid white light means that your device has a Wi-Fi connection.

A solid orange light means there is no Wi-Fi connection. A blinking orange light means that your device is connected to Wi-Fi but cannot access Alexa.

Microphone off Button

Found at the top of Echo is the microphone off button. When pressed this allows you to turn off the Echo's seven microphones. On doing this the light ring will turn red.

Action Button

Similarly found on top of Echo is the action button which wakes Alexa. Use this to also turn off a timer, an alarm and put Echo into Wi-Fi setup mode if held for five seconds.

Volume Ring

By turning the volume ring clockwise Alexa's volume will increase, turn counter-clockwise for the volume to decrease. The light ring will display the volume level.

Bluetooth Settings

Echo comes built with Bluetooth compatibility which means you can connect to your mobile device by simply using the command *"Pair"*. Ensure that the Bluetooth on your mobile device is activated and in Echo's range before you request Alexa to pair. Alexa will notify you once you have successfully paired. To disconnect say *"Disconnect"*. It's that easy!

Using Multiple Devices

At this time there is no way to connect Alexa enabled devices so that they perform the same function. However using the Alexa App you can manage up to 12 different Alexa-enabled devices. So long as each one is registered to your Amazon account. Here are some helpful tips on how to use multiple Alexa-enabled devices.

For Echo and Echo Dot -choose different wake words for devices that are installed within speaking range of each other. If different devices have the same wake word make sure that they are at least 30 feet apart. Use the Alexa App or the Voice Remote for Amazon Echo to request/command one specific device.

For Fire TV Devices and Amazon Tap- give each device a distinct name.

Content sharing across Alexa devices is an areas which does require some improvement from Amazon. Currently you can view all the content which is shared between devices on the Alexa App in the settings menu. But, you are unable to customize which content is available to which device. Content that is shared across your Amazon account includes:

- Flash briefing
- Household profiles
- Music and media
- Shopping
- Smart Home Devices
- To Do Lists

Content that is not shared across your Amazon account includes:

- Alarms
- Bluetooth connections
- Sounds
- Wake Words

Software Updates

Alike all pieces of software, Alexa updates should be expected and continuously looked for. Before downloading the latest software you should check which version you have installed. To do this:

Open Alexa App > Open the left hand side navigation panel > Choose *Settings* > Select your device > Scroll down until *Device Software Version* is displayed.

To download the most recent software update ensure that your Echo is switched on and has an active Wi-Fi connection. Then, avoid requesting/commanding anything from your device whilst the new software installs.

The light ring will turn blue once the update is ready to be installed. The time it takes to install the software update will vary and can depend on the speed of your Wi-Fi connection.

Chapter 2: All About Alexa

Alexa is a cloud-based, voice recognition software. Activated using your desired wake word, you can ask Alexa a question such as *"What is the weather in London today?"* Or you can ask Alexa to do something like *"Add olives to my shopping*

list" or *"play Coldplay's new album"*. You can even connect Alexa to your smart home devices and control your thermostat, lights, power outlets and more using just Alexa and your voice. For instance you could say *"Alexa, turn off the lights in the bedroom"* and they would turn off.

Just like a search engine you can review your voice interactions with Alexa. To do this: Open Alexa App > Choose Settings (from the left hand side navigation panel) > Select History.

By reviewing your interactions with Alexa you can help to improve how Alexa understands. You can also give feedback on inaccurate translations through the Alexa App.

In the same location of the Alexa App you can also delete voice interactions with Alexa from your History. To do this, tap an entry and the choose *Delete.*

The Alexa Skills Kit is free to download and will allow you to personalize and extend your Echo experience beyond all limits. If you want to access Alexa skills that have been developed and published you can view, enable and disable them all by visiting the Alexa App. It is also worth noting that in the *Skills* section of the Alexa App you can access a whole host of information about a skill, from invocation phrases, to developer details.

Here's a list of **questions** you can ask Alexa:

> ➤ *"Alexa, what is the weather here tomorrow?"*

> *"Alexa, when is Mother's Day this year?"*
> *"Alexa, what is fifteen times twelve?"*
> *"Alexa, what is capital of Zimbabwe?"*
> *"Alexa, how far is Jupiter?"*
> *"Alexa, who was the first President of America?"*
> *"Alexa, how old is Morgan Freeman?"*
> *"Alexa, who wrote Harry Potter?"*
> *"Alexa, who is the lead singer of Coldplay?"*
> *"Alexa, what is the IMDB rating for Game of Thrones?"*
> *"Alexa, how far is London from here?"*
> *"Alexa, Wikipedia: "Angelina Jolie"*

Get Weather Forecasts

Alexa uses AccuWeather for the latest weather information and can provide this to you dependent on your location.

To begin, you need to set up the location of your Alexa Device. Open the Alexa App > Open the left hand side navigation panel > Select *Settings* > Choose your device > Select *Edit* in *Device Location* > Enter the address > Select *Save*.

Once your location is set up you can ask Alexa:

> *"Alexa, what's the weather?"*
> *"Alexa, what's the weather for this week/day/weekend?"*
> *"Alexa, will it rain tomorrow?"*

You can also ask Alexa about the weather in another location, to do this ask:

> *"Alexa, what's the weather in [city, county, state, country]?"*

Get News Updates

To hear the latest news simply ask Alexa:

> *"Alexa, what's in the news"*

Get Traffic Updates

Alexa can help you to plan your journey, giving you estimated journey lengths and finding you the quickest route depending on the current traffic status.

Firstly Open the Alexa App > Open the left hand side navigation panel > Select *Settings* > Choose *Traffic* > Select *Change address* in the *To* and *From* sections > Click *Save Changes.*

Once you have set your destination you can ask Alexa:

> *"Alexa, how is the traffic?"*
> *"Alexa, what's the traffic like right now?"*
> *"Alexa, what's my commute?"*

Your Calendar

Alexa can not only add events to your calendar but also recall events that both you and others shared with your calendar. To do this you will first need to link you Google account to Alexa through the Alexa App.

> *"Alexa, what's on my calendar?"*
> *"Alexa, what's on my calendar Monday?"*
> *"Alexa, when is my next event?"*
> *"Alexa, add Go Swimming with Jane to my calendar for Monday, July 8th at 8pm.*

Search for Nearby Places

Alexa uses your device location and Yelp to find services that are located nearby you. Before you can use this feature you will need to make sure your device location is accurate. To do this:

Open the Alexa App > Open the left hand side navigation panel > Select *Settings* > Choose *Traffic* > Select *Change address* in the *To* and *From* sections > Click *Save Changes.*

Once your location is set you can ask Alexa to search for a variety of businesses, restaurants and shops. Ask Alexa for the address, phone number and hours of business for nearby places and more. For instance you could say:

> *"Alexa, what businesses are nearby?"*
> *"Alexa, find the address for the nearby [restaurant/business name]"*
> *"Alexa, find the opening hours for the nearby [restaurant/business name]"*
> *"Alexa, how far is [restaurant/business name]?"*
> *"Alexa, what is the phone number for [restaurant/business name]?"*

Setting Your Alarms and Timers

Alexa allows you to set timers and multiple one-off and repeating alarms. To set, confirm and cancel timers and alarms ask Alexa:

> ➤ *"Alexa, set alarm for 6 am?"*
> ➤ *"Alexa, when is my alarm set for?"*
> ➤ *"Alexa, what time is it?"*
> ➤ *"Alexa, set the timer for 15 minutes"*
> ➤ *"Alexa, how much time is left on my timer?"*
> ➤ *"Alexa, cancel my alarm for tomorrow"*

You can also use Alexa to stop or snooze your alarm when it goes off. To do this say:

> ➤ *"Alexa, stop"*
> ➤ *"Alexa, snooze"*

You can determine the volume and tone of your timer and alarms through the Alexa App. Firstly > Open the Alexa App > Open the left hand navigation panel > Select *Settings* > Chose your device > Select *Sounds* > Chose *Alarm and Timer Volume.*

Managing Lists

Alexa can help you keep organized. With the ability to list up to 100 items on each list, you can view your lists on your desktop, (the Amazon website), the Alexa App and even print them out.

To **open a list** > Open the mobile Alexa App > Open the left hand side navigation panel > Select *Shopping and To-Do Lists* > Select your desired list and view.

You can request Alexa to **review and add items** to your existing lists by saying:

> ➢ *"Alexa, what's on my To-Do List?"*
> ➢ *"Alexa, what's on my Shopping List?"*
> ➢ *"Alexa, add [item] to my Shopping list."*
> ➢ *"Alexa, put [task] onto my To-do List."*

In the Alexa App you can also **mark items as complete** to do this > Open the Alexa App > Open the left hand side navigation menu > Select *Shopping and To-Do Lists* > Choose the list you want > Select a checkbox next to an item.

To **view only your completed items** > Open the Alexa App > Open the left hand side navigation menu > Select *Shopping and To-Do Lists* > Choose the list you want > Select *View Completed*.

To **print a list** > Open the Alexa App on your desktop > Open the left hand side navigation menu > Select *Shopping and To-Do Lists* > Choose the list you want to print > Select *Print* > Follow the instructions provided by your web browser.

Smart Home Devices

Alexa can integrate with a number of smart home devices. Devices that Alexa can operate include; lights, fans, thermostats, doors, locks, power outlets and appliances. To use a smart home device with Alexa ensure that you follow the instructions and recommendations that are given by the device manufacture.

Before connecting your smart home device with Alexa, download the companion app > Set up the smart home device so that is uses the same Wi-Fi network as Alexa > Ensure that your device is running the latest software.

To connect your smart home device with Alexa you will need to:

Open the Alexa app > Open the left hand navigation panel > Choose *Skills* > Select *Refine* > Choose *Smart Home Skills* > Search for the skill your smart home device requires > Select *Enable* > Sign in using your third party log in details (details for the smart device) if required > Save > Say "Alexa, discover my devices" or select *Discover devices* from the Alexa App.

Once you have linked your smart home device with Alexa you can control and operate it using your voice by saying:

> *"Alexa, turn on [smart home device name]"*
> *"Alexa, turn off [smart home device]"*

> *"Alexa, set brightness to [?]%"* - This can only be used with compatible lights that allow you to change the brightness.
> *"Alexa, set [thermostat name] temperature to [?] degrees"*
> *"Alexa, raise/lower the [thermostat name/room name] temperature"*
> *"Alexa, turn the lights on in [room name]"*
> *"Alexa, turn the fan on in [room name]"*
> *"Alexa, set the fan to [?]%"*

By using the Alexa Skills Kit you can create skills that will integrate your smart home device with Alexa - should skills not be available for your requirements. To find smart home skills that are available to you and your device:

Open the Alexa App > Open the left hand side navigation panel > Select *Skills* > Choose *Refine* > Select *Smart Home Skills*.

Chapter 3: An Introduction To Echo's Main Features

Straight out of the box the Amazon Echo is primed and ready for use. Once the quick setup has been completed, Alexa is waiting for instructions.

Let's explore some of the main features of the Echo and, likely, the ones you'll use most often.

As the lower half of the Echo's cylinder is a speaker, let's start with its music and streaming options.

Music:

The Amazon Echo can connect to a variety of music streaming services, including: iHeart Radio, Spotify, Pandora, Amazon Music, Amazon Prime and tunein. It's still early days for the Amazon Echo, but plans to expand its streaming services are in the pipeline.

To play a single track: give Alexa the track name (for added accuracy, it's a good idea to include the name of the artist as well) and proceed it with the word "Play". Alexa will connect to the streaming services and browse through your playlists to find the track you requested.

For example: if you'd like to listen to "Bohemian Rhapsody", say: "Alexa, play 'Bohemian Rhapsody'." To ensure that the echo finds the correct track and not a cover or remix, say: "Alexa, play "Bohemian Rhapsody" by Queen."

You can also tell Alexa to play a single artist or band, and Alexa will shuffle all tracks by that artist or band from across the streaming services. You can pause; rewind, replay, skip and fast-forward tracks by using the appropriate command: "Alexa, pause." "Alexa, rewind track." "Alexa, replay..." Just remember to always precede each command with: Alexa.

You can select just one genre of music and Alexa will scan the streaming services to locate the genre you requested. For example: if you'd like to hear some classical music, say: "Alexa, play classical music," and Alexa will locate classical music playlists and tracks for you. You can also navigate through the selection with voice-commands like the ones above.

You can instruct Alexa to play "Today's hits" from Pandora and if you hear a song you like, you can tell Alexa to get information about that track and download it. It's also possible to select your preferred radio show from iHeartradio, as well as other stations via your handheld devices.

In addition to the available streaming services, the Amazon Echo can access other music platforms––like iTunes––from other devices such as iPhones, androids and tablets. This hands-free approach to playing music is very convenient––especially if your somebody who likes to listen to music whilst cooking, cleaning or other activities that make it difficult for you to use your phone or music device manually. It's also a fantastic option for people who struggle with mobility issues or have limited eyesight.

Podcasts and Audio Books:

The Amazon Echo can access podcasts and live streams on request, as long as they're available on the streaming services. You can command Alexa to play your favorite podcasts and even ask her to catch up on missed episodes. As with music, Alexa can pause, skip and rewind any podcast.

If you have an Audible or Kindle account, you can ask Alexa to find the latest "must-reads", critically acclaimed books, or pick up from where you left off in your favorite page-turner––all without the hassle of scrolling through menus and browsers. Alexa can locate chapters, page numbers and even specific line numbers if you'd like to re-read that riveting sentence, or if you missed it, or if you simply need to pick up from where you left off.

The Echo features a voice-purchase service that allows you to buy music via voice-command. If you hear a track that's to your liking, you can ask to buy that track and/or the entire album. Tell Alexa: "Alexa, shop for song..." "Alexa, shop for Album..." Or "Alexa, shop for artist..." Alexa will confirm with you before it purchases the track or album using the "1-Click" method from the Amazon Digital Music store. Additionally, Amazon Prime members can add songs to their library at no cost.

Flash Briefing/News, Weather, Traffic and Sport:

The Amazon Echo can give you the news of the day with its "Flash Briefing" feature. Initially, the Amazon Echo sourced most of its news information from NPR, ESPN and the BBC. However, the flash briefing feature has expanded it's range of sources to include: CNN, Huffington Post, Fox Sport, Bloomberg, TMZ, The Economist and more. To get your daily Flash Briefing, say: "Alexa, what's my Flash Briefing?" and the Echo shall play a pre-recorded news summery. The default news source is NPR, but this can be changed via the Alexa app.

Open the Alexa app: in the navigation menu, scroll down to "Settings" and select "Flash Briefing". A panel will open listing all available news sources. On the right hand side of the panel there is a toggle ON/OFF option for each news source. Simply adjust to your preference and the next time you ask Alexa for a Flash Briefing, the Echo will give you a flash briefing from your preferred news source.

To get a weather updates or weather warnings: log into the Alexa app and select "Settings", find "Device Location", select "Edit", enter your address and click "Save". The Echo is now set to your location.

Ask Alexa: "Alexa, what's the weather?" And Alexa will give you a detailed summery of the current weather at your location and what to expect for the rest of the day––you can also request a seven-day forecast. Alexa uses AccuWeather to source reliable weather updates and alerts. In addition to local weather updates, this feature can provide a weather update from almost anywhere in the world. Just ask Alexa what the weather is like in whichever city you please, and Alexa will tell you what that city's current weather is as well as what's forecasted for the rest of the day, and––if you're interested––the rest of the week.

Should you require a traffic summery––ask Alexa: "What's the traffic like?" and Alexa will provide you with a detailed assessment of the traffic conditions for your journey, giving you the chance to plan ahead and avoid heavy traffic.

To get updates on your favorite sports teams, locate the "Sports Update" feature under Settings in the Alexa app. The Sports Update feature allows you to customize sports updates based of your preferred team or player by adding their names to the list. Once you've chosen your preferred teams and players, you can receive updates about them by asking Alexa for your sports update. You can also check the progress of teams by asking Alexa a specific question such as: "Alexa, what was the result of the Giants game?" And "Alexa, who do the Yankees play against next?"

Personal Organization:

The Amazon Echo is certainly among the very best devices on the market to offer personal organization options. From alarms and shopping lists; the Amazon Echo can streamline your hectic schedule into a simple set of alerts and reminders. Also, the Echo does away with the manual entry of diary information and to-do lists. All your plans can be stored and organized simply by telling Alexa the important details and she will remind you when an important event is nearing—freeing your mind from planning anxieties.

To set an alarm with the Amazon Echo, just tell Alexa to set an alarm for the time you need. You can tell Alexa to cancel the alarm and, if required, to reset it for another time. To stop the alarm: tell Alexa to "Stop". If you'd like to sleep-in, you can tell Alexa to delay the alarm by saying: "Snooze." Follow the same process to set a timer or a stopwatch.

Need to know the time? Ask Alexa and she'll tell you precisely. If you need to know the time somewhere else in the world, ask Alexa: "Alexa, what time is it in..." and she'll give you the exact time of that location.

The Amazon Echo can sync with your Google Calendar via the Alexa app: Select "Settings", "Calendar" and finally "Link Google calendar account." Once synched, you can check your calendar by voice-command and Alexa will notify you of your plans for that day, that week or the whole month. Not sure if you're free to attend that party on the 20th? Ask Alexa if you have any plans on that day, if not––tell her to reserve the 20th for the party.

You can create shopping and to-do lists with the Amazon Echo. These lists are also saved to the app where items can be manually edited or deleted, or you could ask Alexa to edit or delete them instead of using the app. Items can be added to your shopping list simply by asking Alexa to add the item you require to your list. To remove an item: command Alexa to remove the item that you no longer need, and Alexa will adjust your list in the app accordingly.

The Echo can access Wikipedia, as well as other online services, to find you quick answers to questions. Tell Alexa to give you the date of a national holiday, then if you'd like to know more about that holiday––ask Alexa to Wikipedia it.

If you need the correct spelling of a particular word, Alexa can help you––just ask her for the correct spelling.

The Echo is now connected to Yelp, so you can ask Alexa about local restaurants and businesses. You can also ask Alexa to rate each business, tell you their opening times and see which establishment is most recommended. Just make sure that you have correctly entered your address in the Alexa app.

Streaming Music Services

With Echo you can also listen to streaming music services. These include Spotify Premium, iHeartRadio and Pandora. Before you can play music from your streaming service and through Alexa you will need to link these services together. To do this:

Open Alexa App > Open the left hand side navigation panel > Choose *Music and Books* > Choose your streaming service from the options > Select *Link account to Alexa* > Sign into your account (using the login details you signed up to your music streaming service with) > Once you have logged in Alexa and your music streaming service should be connected.

If your account fails to connect try resetting your login details and then linking your account to Alexa again.

To **unlink your account** > Open the Alexa App > Open the left hand side navigation panel > Choose *Music and Books* > Choose your streaming service from the options > Select Unlink

Once you have successfully linked your account with Alexa you can request Alexa to stream music at your leisure. To this you will need the following commands:

➤ Play Prime Music - *"Play Prime Music"*

➢ Play Spotify Premium - *"Play Spotify Premium"*
➢ Play a radio station - *"Play [station frequency]"* or *"Play [station name]"*
➢ Play a custom station - *"Play my [artist/genre] station on [Pandora/iHeartRadio/Prime Music]"*
➢ Play a podcast or program - *"Play the podcast [podcast name]/"* or *"Play the program [program name]"*
➢ Skip to the next song - *"Skip"*
➢ Like / Dislike a song - *"I like this song /I don't like this song"* or *"Thumbs up/ Thumbs down"*
➢ Take a frequently played song off the playlist/out of rotation (Pandora and Prime Stations only) - *"I'm tired of this song"*

Buying Music

Not only can you play music from your music library and stream music from your streaming service but now with Alexa you can also purchase music. If you have a valid U.S billing address and U.S bank issued or U.S Amazon.com Gift Card you can access this service. Unfortunately, at this time this service is not available to people that do not meet this requirements.

Note: Before you can begin shopping you will first need to update your **voice purchasing settings**. See Chapter 4 for how to do this.

Brought to you through Amazon's Digital Music Store you can purchase music and pay using Echo's 1-click payment method. Purchases that you make from the Digital Music Store are saved in your music library and don't count toward storage limits. Plus, purchases can be played back as much or as little as like and you can also access and download them onto any device that supports Amazon Music.

To edit the settings that enable, disable and identify whether you require a confirmation code for purchasing > Open the Alexa App > Open the left hand side navigation panel > Choose *Settings* > Select *Voice* > Choose *Purchasing*.

Alexa will always notify you of any additional costs when purchasing music.

Once you have set Echo up to purchase music for you through the Alexa App you will need the following commands:

> To shop for a song or album - *"Shop for the song [song name]"*
> To shop for songs by a particular artist - *"Shop for songs by [artists name]"*
> To purchase the song currently playing - *"Buy this [song/album]"*
> To add the song currently playing to your playlist - *"Add this [song/album] to my library"*

Chapter 4: Spotlight on Shopping

Just as you can ask Alexa to play music you can ask Alexa to help you with your shopping. For all aspects of shopping through Alexa you will need an Amazon account.

Currently you can only purchase items through Amazon.com. This can be items you have previously purchased, items that are top Prime products and digital music and albums.

Before you can begin shopping you will first need to update your **voice purchasing settings**. Note, that by default voice purchasing is set to 'on'. To do this:

Open the Alexa App > Open the left hand side navigation panel > Choose *Settings* > Select *Voice Purchasing*.

> ➤ Toggle the *Purchase by voice* option to turn voice purchasing on or off.

➢ You can enable *Require confirmation code*, this means that you will need to supply a 4-digit confirmation code before each and every order > Enter a 4-digit code > Select *Save Changes*. Although you will have to supply your 4-digit code by voice before purchasing it will not appear in your voice history.

➢ From the *Voice Purchasing* settings you can also manage 1-click settings, to do this select *Go To Amazon.com* and set your payment method and billing address.

To purchase **Physical Products** you will need to have previously ordered them from Amazon.com. You will also need an annual membership or 30-day free trial of Amazon Prime.

Once Alexa has found the item you will then need to confirm or cancel the order. If Alexa finds two items which fulfill the request, Alexa will offer the second item after you have declined the first.

If Alexa can't find an item in your history Alexa might offer you an item from Amazon's Choice. Amazon's Choice is a list of items that have high ratings and are well priced with Prime shipping.

If Alexa can't find your item and doesn't offer you an Amazon's Choice, Alexa will add the item you requested to your Amazon.com shopping list account.

If you have multiple orders waiting to be delivered, Alexa will give you the information of the order that is closest to being delivered.

Some of the commands you need to purchase and re-order items through Amazon are:

- ➢ To reorder an item - *"Reorder [item name]"* or *"Yes/No"* when Alexa asks you to confirm the product found.
- ➢ To add an item to your shopping cart - *"Add [item name] to my cart"*
- ➢ To track the status of an order that has recently been shipped - *"Track my order"* or *"Where is my stuff"*
- ➢ To cancel an order - *"Cancel my order"* - Note you can only do this immediately after you have confirmed an order.

Remember that you can always visit Amazon.com on your mobile device or desktop to confirm, edit and cancel any orders you make through Alexa should you need to.

Returns

The full return policy for products purchased through Alexa can be found at:

https://www.amazon.com/gp/help/customer/display.html?nodeId=15015721

Non-digital products that are purchased using Alexa are automatically eligible for free returns. If you accidently purchase a song or album from the Amazon Digital Music Store you can request a return and refund but, your request must be received by Amazon Customer Service within seven days.

Chapter 5: Extras

1. Access Echo Online

Yes, the Alexa App is quick, simple and very easy to access but if for whatever reason you can't access the Alexa App just visit http://echo.amazon.com

2. Ask Alexa Funny Questions

Just alike other voice recognition software you can ask Alexa a variety of questions to which Alexa will respond with comical and witty answers. Try out these:

➤ *"Alexa, is Santa real?"*

➤ *"Alexa, what is love?"*

➤ *"Alexa, I want the truth?"*

➤ *"Alexa, is this the real life?"*

➤ *"Alexa, I have a cold?"*

➤ *"Alexa, you complete me"*

➤ *"Alexa, to be or not to be?"*

3. The Alexa App

The Alexa App is the go-to tool to help you set up Echo and Alexa. Available on your mobile device and through your desktop and web browser Alexa has everything you need to customize and control Alexa hands on.

Here is a short list of what each feature in the Alexa App navigation panel does.

Note: To find the navigation panel > Open the Alexa App > On the left hand side if a Menu icon > Select this.

> Help and Feedback - Here you will find in depth help information for your Echo device. You can also submit feedback about your experience with Alexa, good or bad.

> Home - Show you your voice history with Alexa

> Music and Books - This allows you to search for songs, radio stations, shows, Kindle Books and audiobooks that you can listen to through Echo.

> Now Playing - Shows you the track you are currently playing, the tracks that are upcoming and the ones previously played.

> Not [Name]? Sign Out - Click here to sign out of the Alexa App

> Settings - In this sub section you will find everything you need to set up your Echo device, you will find various Alexa device settings and you can train Alexa

to understand your speech patterns and annunciations.

➢ Shopping & To Do Lists - Here you can view, manage and edit your shopping and to-do lists.

➢ Skills - You can search for, enable and disable skills that you want Alexa to possess. You can also view all the information about skills from invocation phrases to developer details.

➢ Smart Home - Here you can manage all the settings you need to for smart home devices that you want to/have linked to Alexa.

➢ Times and Alarms - You can view, edit and delete timers and alarms set by Alexa,

➢ Things to Try - Here you will find a list of example phrases that you can ask Alexa.

Chapter 6: Smart Home Controller, "Skills" and Other Features

Along with the Amazon Echo's main features, it's also designed to receive regular updates and run new apps; securing it as a highly adaptable device that will stay up-to-date with similar and new technology. With Alexa operating via the cloud, the Amazon Echo updates automatically and thus ensures that your Echo is fully equipped with the latest features and apps.

The Amazon Echo development team is regularly putting out new features and improving the Echo's compatibility with other well-known services and apps. Apps, or "Skills" as they're known the Echo world (because unlike apps, Skills are stored in the cloud and so don't require downloading), can be fully customized to suit your needs and deliver what you want from your Amazon Echo. As long as The Echo is connected to Wi-Fi, it'll stay up-to-date with the newest features and learn more about you as a user.

To access more: create an account on "If This Then That" (IFTTT). IFTTT is an online tool that allows users to connect websites, apps, platforms and services using the IFTTT algorithm. Users create "Recipes" which is a link between sites or devices or services—these are called channels. Essentially; the "This" part of the abbreviation refers to a "trigger" which in turn triggers an "action"—"That". Actions can be performed across many online services: from social media to file sharing. The trigger is an operation that takes place on one platform that's also linked to another platform. So when something is triggered from one channel; say a user posts a photo to Facebook: the channel connected to Facebook—say twitter—will notice this operation and perform a dedicated action—such as tweeting the same picture uploaded to Facebook, on it's own platform as dictated by the user's recipe. With the IFTTT connection you can create a custom voice commands to work with a multitude of different devices.

To begin connecting your Amazon Echo to other devices you'll need to create an IFTTT account. After you've set up your account, locate the "My Recipes" tap on your IFTTT profile. On loading the recipes window, click on the plus/add/+ symbol at the top right of the screen and wait for the IFTTT browser to load various app options. The "Create a Recipe" tab will appear at the bottom of the screen, selecting this will take you to a page that'll display the text:

"If + then +". A small tab with the text "Start here!" will appear above the first + button. This button takes you to a selected services page. Locate the Alexa app and tap the icon; this will set the Alexa app as the first channel in your recipe and will offer a list of voice-commanded trigger options. Depending on which device or channel you want to connect to––you can scroll down the list to find the best option of voice-commands to set as a trigger. Alternatively, there's a "Say a Specific Phrase" option, which you can customize to fit your trigger. Once you've chosen a phrase for your trigger, select: "Done". You'll then be taken to the next menu: which is the "Then That" or the action option. By clicking the + tab you'll be offered a selection of services or channels that you can connect your Alexa with and use the trigger phrase to have that action perform a specific action.

With IFTTT you can connect your Amazon Echo to a range of social media platforms, calendars and email accounts. Simply create a recipe, using the process above, to

Smart Home Controller:

The Amazon Echo is a perfect controller for smart home devices. Compatible with WeMo, Wink, Philips Hue, Samsung SmartThings and other smart home devices: you can control your lighting, heating and other appliances by voice command. You can control any of these compatible devices using the Alexa app. Ask Alexa to: "Locate new devices" and the Echo will sync with them and provide available control options in the Alexa app. For some smart devices that aren't yet compatible, but available on IFTTT, you can still connect them to Echo and control them. Using IFTTT, connect Alexa to a device and create a recipe and trigger phrase by which to operate that device. Simply follow the process above and select the appropriate options.

With IFTTT integration you can use the Echo to open and close your Garage door using the Garageio app that connects to your garage door system. Again, follow the recipe procedure above to connect Alexa and Garageio. You can also use the Echo to control your TVs, Thermostats, door locks and a great deal more. If you have Automatic's car adaptor––a device that connects to your car's diagnostic port and Bluetooth––which monitors your gas usages, mileage, maintenance issues, GPS etc. You can connect it to the Echo using IFTTT which allows you to ask Alexa how much fuel you have in your tank, how many miles can your car manage with he gas it has and so on. IFTTT and Echo integration offers boundless possibilities when it comes to controlling your home hands-free. Smart home automation controlled by buttons is limited, but the Echo brings forth so many new ways to connect with your home and office.

Popular Skills Recently Added:

To order an Uber, add the Uber app to your skills list in the Alexa app, add your address and follow the prompts to connect to your Uber account. Once the skill has been added to the skills list, and you're ready to use it––tell Alexa to ask Uber for a ride. If there's an Uber car available, Alexa will inform you how far away it is and will ask you if you'd like to order the Uber. You can cancel an Uber anytime via voice command and Alexa will inform the driver. Booking details will also be sent to your Uber app. You can also command Alexa to find the cheapest Uber fare by instructing her to ask Uber to locate the nearest Uber X. And you can check-in in your Uber by asking: "Alexa, how far away is my Uber?"

You can use the Amazon Echo to order pizza using the Dominos skill. In the Alexa app, open "settings" and find "skills". Search for the Dominos skill, add it to the skill list and check that it's enabled. To order pizza, instruct Alexa to ask Dominos that you'd like to order a pizza. Alexa will ask what you'd like to order. Once you've placed your order, Alexa will check to confirm your selection, once you've confirmed Alexa will give you the price of your order. Confirm the order and Alexa will send it to your nearest Dominos pizza place.

If you're a movie Buff, or just fancy a night out at the movies, you can ask: "Alexa, what movies are playing?" And Alexa will scan theatres in your area and list the movies showing that day. To find times of a specific movie, ask: "Alexa, what time is...showing?" Alexa will then list the showing times at theatres in your area. If you'd like to know more about a movie, ask: "Alexa, tell me more about..." You can also find out what other movies are playing, and at what time in different theatres for the rest of the week.

A popular, recent skill now available is the Campbell's recipe app. It's now possible to get help from Alexa while cooking--the benefits of hands-free virtual assistance is obvious. Simply ask Alexa to access Campbell's recipes, and you can search through hundreds of recipes and find new and tasty ways to improve your favorite dish or even try something completely new. You can also find more options and cooking services on IFTTT.

Those few examples barely scratch the surface of the plethora of Skills available. The virtue of being a cloud-based system is that the Amazon Echo allows third party

Chapter 7: Everything the Echo Can Do

As mentioned before, the Echo connects to Alexa, and when asked, it plays music, provides information, sports scores, news, weather, reads audiobooks, and much more. But there is a lot more to the Echo.

With the Echo, people will be able to control music from Amazon Music, Prime Music, Pandora, iHeartRadio, and TuneIn. In addition, the speaker can be used through Bluetooth, allowing users to stream other music from services like iTunes or Spotify through their phone or tablet. With the inclusion of Echo's speakers producing 360-degree omni-directional audio to fill any room with immersive sound, the Echo delivers a nice dynamic bass response.

When first using the Echo, Amazon provides an introductory video and recommendations in the Things to Try section, which gives a variety of commands for the users to learn and test out with the Echo. Amazon also includes a list of topics that range from everything that is listed in the app like alarms, lists, music, and also facts, weather, and general commands such as "Stop," "Cancel," and "Repeat." The app also features suggestions of voice commands to test with the Echo, and new features have been added to the Echo since its first launch.

One of the neatest things about Amazon Echo is that it works well with Smart Home devices such as WeMo, Phillips Hue, Samsung SmartThings, Wink, and Insteon. The Echo could be used to switch the lamp on or off, turn the fan or space heater on, dim the lights in order to set the mood for a perfect movie night, turn off the TV, and even control the thermostat. Anyone could do all this with their Echo without having to lift a finger or get up on their feet. The sound of a person's voice has the ability to make their garage close without them having to leave their favorite spot on the couch. It can play the most recent episode on a favorite podcast. It can even check over math problems.

Echo is capable of reading off weather forecasts, setting timers and alarms, and managing to-do lists and shopping lists. Echo can also cross out items on shopping lists by making purchases on Amazon when Alexa is asked to. And when asked the news, Alexa will give a list of the day's most popular headlines and provide a list of reliable sources such as CNN, Fox Sports Radio, NPR, and BBC News. The owner will have the option to choose which source they want to hear from and which categories they want to hear about. In addition, whenever Echo has more information than it can say through sound, the owner will be referred to a companion Echo app that can also control the Echo through a mobile device, tablet, or web.

To most people, Echo could be portrayed as for entertainment use and convenience, but it is very helpful to individuals who are overcoming disability issues. It gives individuals with disabilities a greater control of their environment and it allows them to be more independent. With people that are bound to a wheelchair, the Echo acts as a lifeline and it enables them to have a normal life. They could create shopping lists, to-do lists, timers, and alarms for when they're undergoing self-therapy, and much more. Doctors and therapists actually recommend Amazon Echo to their patients in an attempt to make their lives easier when they're trying to recover.

The newest version of Amazon Echo has upgrades that everyone will love. People will now be able to order pizza from Domino's, request a ride from the Uber car service, and even get recipes from Campbell's Kitchen. This is possible through third-party developments that Amazon has opened Echo up to known as "Skills." Skills are voice-based apps that can be enabled through a smartphone or tablet app. Skills have apps that have many uses, such as Garageio, which opens the garage, and TV Shows, which can tell one what time an episode of anyone's favorite TV show comes on.

And for the hack-minded individuals, Amazon has added a new feature that will enable the Echo to be used in conjunction with If This, Then That (IFTTT). This will allow Echo to integrate with Evernote, Gmail, Twitter, even phone calls, and a variety of other services, but what can be done with them is very limited. Most of the IFTTT hacks involve controlling the shopping or to-do lists on Echo and using them for other purposes. For instance, IFTTT could set to send every item on Echo's to-do list to a pre-determined recipient in a text message.

Amazon has also added "Ask My Buddy" to the Echo. It allows owners to register for an account and add up to five contacts. Each contact can have an email address, text address/cell phone, and voice phone. When "ask my buddy" is said, the Echo will immediately ask who is the desired person wanted to be contacted. Owners can contact an individual or everyone on the list, and Ask My Buddy will instantly send an alert to those requested. Owners can contact people at a maximum of 120 times a month. This includes each person, text, and email.

The Echo is even perfect when it comes to business matters. For instance, if anyone owns their own office, they could use the Echo in an attempt to keep from running out of supplies for everyday use such as pens, papers, toners, printers, and computer screens. Whenever the office is low on supplies, the Echo needs to be informed in order to allow Amazon to fix the problem. And if someone is a chef, they can use the Echo to create shopping lists of needed ingredients for recipes, and it can even be used to calculate measurements for recipes.

Amazon Echo is more than capable of completing commands and answering questions for its owner. Describing what the Echo is capable of is nothing compared to experiencing how it works. It feels at once normal and magical. Once using the Echo starts feeling natural, it will start to feel like it is part of one's life, and that it does more than what it is made to do. But that's because a bond starts to grow with the "assistant."

Amazon Echo is still relatively new, so it's still undergoing improvements and upgrades. Therefore, one should expect the Echo's "to-do list" to expand. And fortunately, the Echo is always connected to the internet so it will update

Chapter 8: How to Give Proper Commands

Giving Alexa commands is actually pretty easy. Especially when they are very simple like the ones listed below:

- "Alexa, find me a Chinese restaurant."

- "Alexa, what's on my calendar today?"

- "Alexa, set a timer for 20 minutes."

- "Alexa, turn down the volume."

- "Alexa, turn on the lights."

- "Alexa, turn off the TV."

- "Alexa, turn the heat to 74 degrees."

However, there are some important details that people need to know when giving Alexa commands.

1. **Always start the command with Alexa.**

   This is important because the Echo needs to know when it is being talked to. Otherwise, it won't be able to perform the task requested or answer any questions.

2. **Specify which music app the music needs to be played from.**

   It's very likely that when a certain song or artist is requested, most people aren't referring to Amazon Music or Prime Music. When a song or artist is requested, the Echo will immediately play tracks from the Amazon Prime Music library. To request music from another music source, this is what needs to be said: "Alexa, play Adele on Spotify," "Alexa, play my Beyoncé station on iHeartRadio," or "Alexa, play 'Today's Hits' on Pandora."

3. **Make sure to refer to the app names on skills.**

   Some requests will have to do with some of the apps that are on Skills. When referring to them, make sure the name of the app is said: "Alexa, ask TV Shows what time does The Walking Dead start?" "Alexa, ask

Campbell's Kitchen for a recipe." "Alexa, ask Automatic if I need gas."

4. **When speaking to the smart home devices, there's no need to say the device's name.**

The smart home devices such as WeMo, SmartThings, and the others are already linked to the Echo. Therefore they act as one and work together. So when the lights are desired to be turned off, just simply say, "Alexa, turn off the lights."

Echo can also deliver jokes when asked upon request. Some jokes are really only for children but there is one joke that everyone should get a kick out of. During the Super Bowl ad for Amazon Echo, the former NFL quarterback Dan Marino, tried to insult Alec Baldwin by saying, "Alexa, how many Oscars has Alec Baldwin won?" And Alexa replies, "Alec Baldwin has won zero Oscars."

But that's not the funny part! Now, if anyone tries to ask Alexa the same question, Alec Baldwin joins the conversation, a neat trick developed by the Echo's engineers:

Alexa: "Alec Baldwin has won—"

Alec Baldwin's voice: "Alexa, stop."

Alexa: "Alec, is that you? I can stop but you've still won no Oscars!"

The current and future owners of this device will enjoy all that the Echo has to offer. In addition, they will love how quickly Alexa obeys commands and answers questions precisely. She has proven to better one's day just by being of service.

Chapter 9: How the Amazon Echo Has Improved Since it was First Launched

The Amazon Echo was first launched on November 12, 2014. At the time, the device wasn't available for everyone. Purchasing the speaker was invite-only, but fortunately on June 23, 2015, it was released to the public. And since then it's been selling like hotcakes!

In the beginning, Echo was not fully opened to developers. At that time, the Echo software development kit was in a private beta. The beta version was available on a limited basis, like the hardware was initially, meaning by invite-only. And at the time the Echo only worked with Phillips Hue and WeMo devices. In addition, the Echo had very little vocabulary.

But Echo has revolutionized greatly since its first release. The Echo started out very basic. It could only obey simple commands, play music on only a few other services besides Amazon Music, and it was only subject to two smart home devices like the ones mentioned above. However, now there are nearly a thousand new features that have been added to the Echo. Some of them have already been mentioned earlier like the "Ask My Buddy" program and IFTTT. But here's additional information on how the Echo has improved.

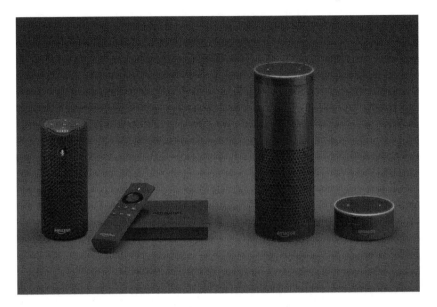

A lot of the new features that have been added to the Echo aren't all of Amazon's doing. Amazon has opened the Echo to other people, allowing any programmer to write new features for it. These features are known as Skills, which was mentioned earlier. Through Skills, anyone can write new features for the Echo that didn't originally come with the device. For example, Spotify! Spotify is now built-in with the Echo and anyone can ask Alexa to play any of their favorite playlists or bands that are listed on their Spotify account. Just make sure that the paid Spotify account address and password are provided on the Alexa App.

In addition, there is Uber. Anyone can now command Alexa to order a car for them just by saying, "Alexa, ask Uber for a ride." From there, Alexa will inform how many minutes away the nearest car is, and then she will ask if the person wants to continue or cancel. The Uber account name and password has to be provided on the Alexa app of course. However, the wording needs to be exact! No one can say, "Call me an Uber," "Order me an Uber," or even "I need an Uber ride." The command has to be "Alexa, ask Uber for a ride." But the good thing about this is that when the car has been ordered, the Uber app on one's phone knows. People will be able to look up the driver's name or license plate, cancel the car, and even track the car on a map.

As mentioned before, anyone can now order pizza with the Echo. All anyone has to do is ask for it out loud. Make sure to set it up right, and everything will be paid for. Except for the tip of course, which could easily be paid to the delivery guy once he comes to the front door. However, setting it up can be a little tricky. Specifying the desired pizza is unlikely, unfortunately. Instead, people will have to re-order a pizza they have previously ordered. They'll have the choice to re-order or Easy Order, which is the favorite size pizza that is stored in the Domino's app. As for the wording, it is fixed, yet simple. To order an Easy Order just simply say, "Alexa, open Domino's and place my Easy Order." The option to define the Easy Order is not available until the order has been placed on the Domino's app for the first time. And then the Echo can be used to order pizza the second time.

For the gamers out there, there are Skills for games such as Minecraft and Destiny that'll make Alexa a worthy sidekick. There are also spoken games such as Bingo and Word Master where players can play against the Echo. For the musicians, there are Skills that allows the Echo to be used as a metronome or guitar tuner. There are even Skills that will teach Alexa to instruct you on how to make cocktail recipes or other types of drinks. Something else that will be found in the Skills section is the variety of smart home products, such as home security systems from Vivint and Scout, the

Garageio smart garage opener, and the Automatic car monitoring gadget. All of which can be voice-controlled.

And for the book readers: when the Echo was first introduced, it was able to play Audible books that were professionally recorded books, which can cost money. Now Alexa can read Kindle books from the library aloud for free. Alexa can even start from where the book was left off. This is very helpful for the very old and the very young. There are also news apps from the Huffington Post, TechCrunch, AOL, and AccuWeather. More apps that feature stock quotes and information on when the next train or bus is coming is also available for use.

The Echo offers futuristic qualities that even a smartphone, tablet, and computer can't display. It has greatly improved since it was first released. And with the help of other developers and programmers, the device continues to update automatically whenever a new feature has been added to it. Fortunately, it continues to improve month after month and delivers satisfaction.

Conclusion

The Echo is very much ahead of its time. Years ago no one expected a device like the Echo to be made until there were flying cars. But it's safe to say that the Amazon Echo is truly extraordinary and that there are no other devices like it. Siri, Cortana, or any other voice service can't compare to the extreme brilliancy that the Echo has to offer.

There is no specified age group that the Echo is recommended for. But the Echo is great for everyone. From babies to the elderly, the Echo is of perfect service. It can be quite a distraction for kids by delivering songs, kids' books, and even telling silly jokes. And it's a great help for the elderly. Especially for the ones who are trying to be independent when they truly can't. But the Echo makes that happen for them.

This guide covers the simplest of set up and gets you going with the skeleton of how Echo works. Starting with plugging in, Wi-Fi connection, Bluetooth pairing and the physical hardware.

To some people, the Echo may seem like a new useless gadget. But to others, it's a breakthrough to making one's day better and easier, especially if they are always busy. Not everyone needs to have the Echo, but one can't help but admit that it is a pretty cool speaker. Where else can anyone find a speaker that can deliver them pizza and order them a car from Uber? It sounds ridiculous, but the engineers and developers at Amazon have made this very likely.

In addition, it is hands-free! Other devices that have voice-control usually require the need for it to be accessed by hitting a specific button and then the voice service pops up. But not with the Amazon Echo. One can literally say "Alexa" and then it is ready to answer any questions or obey any orders that it is given. It acts as an assistant, but in reality, it is more than that. With the Echo, one can mix business and pleasure.

And now, the Amazon Echo has mini versions for people to have just in case they don't want the big one. They are called Echo Dot and Amazon Tap. The Echo Dot is basically the Echo's little sister. It can perform all the tasks and has all the same features that the Echo has. The only difference is that it's smaller and it has the option to hook up to an external speaker. Amazon Tap is a portable, rechargeable Wi-Fi and Bluetooth speaker that uses Alexa to control music, deliver news, get weather reports, and more. But in order to talk to the Tap, a button has to be pressed for Alexa to listen.

Amazon is just full of surprises! Customers are now going to have trouble deciding on which one to purchase. But for them to make the decision easier on themselves, they need to consider the costs and which one is better fitting for their needs. The Echo costs $179.99, the Echo Dot costs $89.99, and the Amazon Tap costs $129.99. These devices are birthed from the same place, and they are all a part of the Amazon Echo family. They just have certain qualities that make them different.

The quiet and modest release of the Echo has exploded into a worldwide frenzy. No wonder when one considers the endless productivity and ease of use that this device offers. The longevity of the Amazon Echo looks firmly secured as manufactures of similar devices are looking closely at this unbeatable competitor. Things are only going to get better for Alexa, it's bright future is assured and it's quality and performance remains unrivalled.

Thank you for reading. I hope you enjoy it. I ask you to leave your honest feedback.

I think next books will also be interesting for you:

Amazon Tap

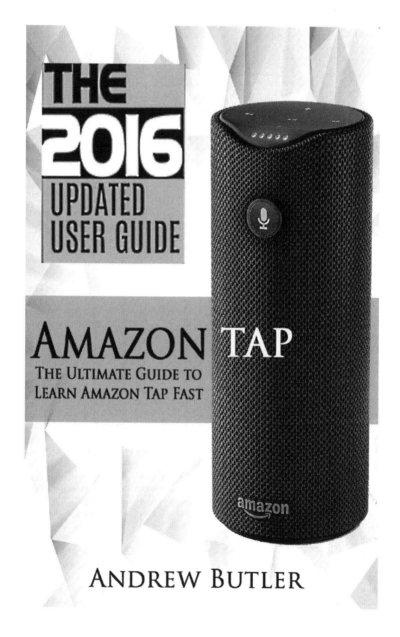

Amazon Dot

Windows 10

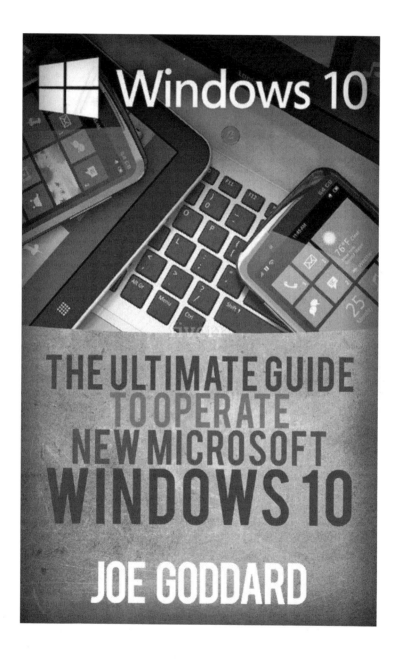

Amazon Fire TV

Amazon Fire TV

Made in the USA
Lexington, KY
05 December 2016